The Empire State Building

Lisa Bullard

Lerner Publications Company
Minneapolis

For Laura,
with hopes that
she'll reach for
the stars
—L.B.

Lerner Publications Company
A division of Lerner Publishing Group, Inc.
241 First Avenue North
Minneapolis, MN 55401 U.S.A.

Website address: www.lernerbooks.com

Library of Congress Cataloging-in-Publication Data

Bullard, Lisa
    The Empire State Building / by Lisa Bullard.
      p.   cm. — (Lightning Bolt Books™—Famous Places)
    Includes index.
    ISBN 978-0-8225-9404-8 (lib. bdg. : alk. paper)
    1. Empire State Building (New York, N.Y.)—Juvenile literature.
    2. New York (N.Y.)—Buildings, structures, etc.—Juvenile literature. I. Title.
    F128.8.E46B85 2010
    974.7'1—dc22   2008030642

Manufactured in the United States of America
1 2 3 4 5 6 — BP — 15 14 13 12 11 10

Contents

Fighting to Be Tallest

The race was on! Who could build the tallest building in the world? Two friends, John J. Raskob and Alfred E. Smith, thought they could.

Raskob (at left) and Smith stand beside a model of the Empire State Building.

The first design for the Empire State Building included a landing area for dirigibles, or airships!

Raskob and Smith decided to build the **Empire State Building in New York City.** They hired planners and builders.

EMPIRE STATE BUILDING · NEW YORK CITY

A man named Walter P. Chrysler had the same idea. He had New York's Chrysler Building built in 1930. It is almost 1,050 feet (320 meters) tall.

For less than one year, the Chrysler Building was the tallest building in the world.

The following year, the Empire State Building was finished. It opened on May 1, 1931. It was the tallest building in the world.

Lots of people gathered for the grand opening of the Empire State Building on May 1, 1931.

Lightning strikes the Empire State Building about one hundred times each year.

The famous skyscraper is 1,250 feet (381 m) tall. Antennas and a lightning rod have been added to the top. They make it 1,454 feet (443 m) tall.

The Empire State Building remained the world's tallest building for more than forty years.

The Empire State Building still towers over most of New York City.

Millions of people visit it every year.

They travel to the 86th or 102nd floor. They can see the city from observatories there.

Observatories allow people to see far-off distances.

Steel columns run all the way around the Empire State Building.

New Inventions

New inventions allowed the Empire State Building to be built. Inventors discovered a way to make steel very quickly. The cost of steel went down. Stronger steel columns and beams were used to support tall skyscrapers. The Empire State Building was one of these.

A worker perches on the end of a giant steel beam.

A total of 210 steel columns hold up the Empire State Building. Steelworkers put in the columns. They worked high up in the open air. Some had no ropes or nets.

A worker hangs onto a cable high above the ground.

Elevators were made safe. People couldn't climb all of the stairs to the 102nd floor of the Empire State Building. But with elevators, people could get there quickly and easily.

The Empire State Building grew taller and taller. At one point, workers added one floor almost every day.

A New Way to Build

Workers built the Empire State Building in record time. They finished it in one year and forty-five days. They did this by using brand-new ideas about building.

Workers rivet a steel beam into place.

Parts of the building were made at other places. Trucks brought the parts to the building site.

A crane picks up building parts from a truck.

Small railroad cars inside the building carried supplies to workers. The workers added the pieces to the building's frame.

Workers pushed railroad cars loaded with supplies over little tracks.

Sometimes the building held more than three thousand workers on the different floors.

Workers built many different floors at the same time. Each new floor made a cover for the one below.

Workers on top floors placed steel beams. Workers on the lower floors could do other jobs, such as painting.

Builders work high above the city streets.

A Special Look

Architect **William Lamb** planned how the building would be built. The skyscraper is 102 stories tall. It has 6,500 windows. The building does not rise in a straight line. It gets narrower as it rises.

The building narrows at the setbacks. A setback is a place where a wall is built back from the edge of a building.

This photo shows some of the Empire State Building's setbacks.

On most nights, the top of the Empire State Building is lit up.

Different colored lights are used for special holidays.

The Empire State Building is lit up with red and green lights for Christmas.

Still Standing Tall

Several newer buildings are taller than the Empire State Building. It has not been the world's tallest since 1972.

People from all over the world come to see the Empire State Building. It remains one of New York City's most popular places.

But the skyscraper remains one of the world's greatest buildings.

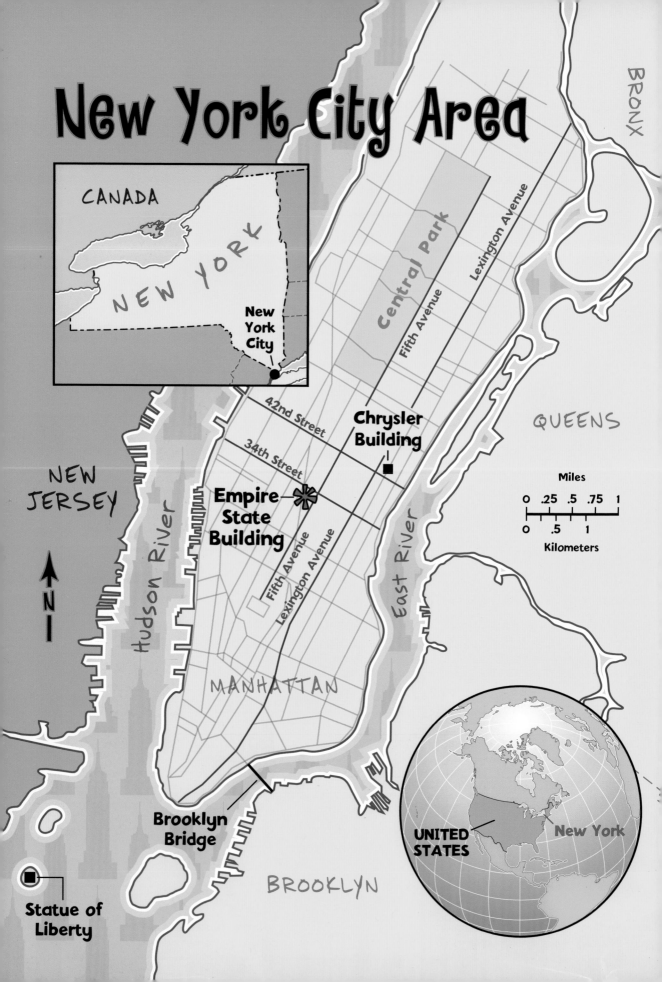

New York City Area

CANADA

NEW YORK

New York City

NEW JERSEY

N

Hudson River

42nd Street

34th Street

Empire State Building

Fifth Avenue

Lexington Avenue

Central Park

Fifth Avenue

Lexington Avenue

Chrysler Building

BRONX

QUEENS

East River

MANHATTAN

Brooklyn Bridge

BROOKLYN

Statue of Liberty

Miles
0 .25 .5 .75 1

0 .5 1
Kilometers

UNITED STATES

New York

Fun Facts

- The Empire State Building gets its name from a nickname for New York—the Empire State.

- Planners thought dirigibles could dock at the top of the building. Then passengers could unload. But early tests showed this plan was not safe.

- In July 1945, an airplane accidentally crashed into the Empire State Building. Fourteen people were killed. The building was damaged. But it was fixed.

- Every year, there is a race inside the Empire State Building. People run up 1,576 steps to the 86th-floor observatory. The record time for reaching the observatory is nine minutes and thirty-seven seconds.

Glossary

antenna: a rod or wire that sends or receives television and radio signals

architect: a person who creates the plans to make a building

dirigible: a large airship that can be steered.

elevator: a machine in a building that moves people up and down

lightning rod: a metal device that helps keep a building from being damaged when hit by lightning

observatory: a place from which you can see far away

rivet: to bind together with rivets, or metal bolts

setback: a place where a wall is built back from the edge of a building, making it narrower

skyscraper: a tall building that is held up by a steel frame

Further Reading

Big Apple History
http://pbskids.org/bigapplehistory/index-flash.html

Building Big: Skyscrapers
http://www.pbs.org/wgbh/buildingbig/skyscraper/index.html

Curlee, Lynn. *Skyscraper.* New York: Atheneum Books for Young Readers, 2007.

Empire State Building
http://www.esbnyc.com/index2.cfm

Hopkinson, Deborah. *Sky Boys: How They Built the Empire State Building.* New York: Schwartz & Wade Books, 2006.

Kirk, Connie Ann. *Sky Dancers.* New York: Lee & Low Books, 2004.

Index

Photo Acknowledgments

The images in this book are used with the permission of: © Mitchell Funk/The Image Bank/Getty Images, pp. 2, 8; AP Photo, pp. 4, 7; © Smithsonian Institution/CORBIS, p. 5; © Mansell/Time & Life Pictures/Getty Images, p. 6; © Marta Johnson, p. 9; © Patti McConville/Photographer's Choice/Getty Images, p. 10; © Steffen Thalemann/Iconica/Getty Images, p. 11; Photography Collection, Miriam and Ira D. Wallach Division of Art, Prints and Photographs, The New York Public Library, Astor, Lenox and Tilden Foundations, pp. 12, 13, 14, 15, 16, 18, 21; Collection of The Skyscraper Museum, p. 19; © Lewis W. Hine/George Eastman House/Hulton Archive/Getty Images, p. 20; © Glowimages/Getty Images, p. 22; © Leanna Rathkelly/Photographer's Choice/Getty Images, p. 23; © Melvin Levine/Time & Life Pictures/Getty Images, p. 24; © Grant Faint/The Image Bank/Getty Images, p. 25; © age fotostock/SuperStock, p. 26; © Karl Kummels/SuperStock, p. 27; © Laura Westlund/Independent Picture Service, p. 28; © Ambient Images Inc./Alamy, p. 30.

Front cover: © Alan Schein Photography/CORBIS.